THE AFRICAN–AMERICAN HEART SURGERY PIONEER

The Genius of Vivien Thomas

Titles in the *Genius Inventors and Their Great Ideas* Series:

The Man Who Invented the Ferris Wheel: The Genius of George Ferris
Library Ed. ISBN: 978-0-7660-4136-3
Paperback ISBN: 978-1-4644-0206-7 • EPUB ISBN: 978-1-4645-1119-6
Single-User PDF ISBN: 978-1-4646-1119-3 • Multi-User PDF ISBN: 978-0-7660-5748-7

The Man Who Invented the Electric Guitar: The Genius of Les Paul
Library Ed. ISBN: 978-0-7660-4137-0
Paperback ISBN: 978-1-4644-0207-4 • EPUB ISBN: 978-1-4645-1120-2
Single-User PDF ISBN: 978-1-4646-1120-9 • Multi-User PDF ISBN: 978-0-7660-5749-4

The Man Who Invented the Laser: The Genius of Theodore H. Maiman
Library Ed. ISBN: 978-0-7660-4138-7
Paperback ISBN: 978-1-4644-0208-1 • EPUB ISBN: 978-1-4645-1121-9
Single-User PDF ISBN: 978-1-4646-1121-6 • Multi-User PDF ISBN: 978-0-7660-5750-0

The Man Who Invented Television: The Genius of Philo T. Farnsworth
Library Ed. ISBN: 978-0-7660-4139-4
Paperback ISBN: 978-1-4644-0209-8 • EPUB ISBN: 978-1-4645-1122-6
Single-User PDF ISBN: 978-1-4646-1122-3 • Multi-User PDF ISBN: 978-0-7660-5751-7

The Woman Who Invented the Thread That Stops Bullets: The Genius of Stephanie Kwolek
Library Ed. ISBN: 978-0-7660-4141-7
Paperback ISBN: 978-1-4644-0211-1 • EPUB ISBN: 978-1-4645-1124-0
Single-User PDF ISBN: 978-1-4646-1124-7 • Multi-User PDF ISBN: 978-0-7660-5753-1

The Man Who Invented the Game of Basketball: The Genius of James Naismith
Library Ed. ISBN: 978-0-7660-4142-4
Paperback ISBN: 978-1-4644-0212-8 • EPUB ISBN: 978-1-4645-1125-7
Single-User PDF ISBN: 978-1-4646-1125-4 • Multi-User PDF ISBN: 978-0-7660-5754-8

GENIUS INVENTORS AND THEIR GREAT IDEAS

THE AFRICAN–AMERICAN HEART SURGERY PIONEER

The Genius of Vivien Thomas

Edwin Brit Wyckoff

Enslow Elementary

an imprint of

Enslow Publishers, Inc.

40 Industrial Road
Box 398
Berkeley Heights, NJ 07922
USA

http://www.enslow.com

Series Literacy Consultant
Allan A. De Fina, Ph.D.
Past President of the New Jersey Reading Association
Professor, Department of Literacy Education
New Jersey City University

Enslow Elementary, an imprint of Enslow Publishers, Inc.
Enslow Elementary® is a registered trademark of Enslow Publishers, Inc.

Library of Congress Cataloging-in-Publication Data

Wyckoff, Edwin Brit.
  The African-American heart surgery pioneer : the genius of Vivien Thomas / by Edwin Brit Wyckoff.
      p. cm.— (Genius inventors and their great ideas)
  Includes index.
  ISBN 978-0-7660-4140-0
  1. Thomas, Vivien T., 1910-1985—Juvenile literature. 2. Surgeons—Maryland—Biography—Juvenile
literature. 3. Cardiovascular system--Surgery--Juvenile literature. I. Title.
  RD27.35.T46W92 2013
  617.4'12092—dc23
  [B]
                                                                    2012013208

Future editions:
Paperback ISBN: 978-1-4644-0210-4
Single-User PDF ISBN: 978-1-4646-1123-0

EPUB ISBN: 978-1-4645-1123-3
Multi-User PDF ISBN: 978-0-7660-5752-4

Printed in the United States of America.
032013 Lake Book Manufacturing, Inc., Melrose Park, IL
10 9 8 7 6 5 4 3 2 1

To Our Readers: We have done our best to make sure all Internet addresses in this book were active and appropriate when we went to press. However, the author and the publisher have no control over and assume no liability for the material available on those Internet sites or on other Web sites they may link to. Any comments or suggestions can be sent by e-mail to comments@enslow.com or to the address on the back cover.

♻ Enslow Publishers, Inc., is committed to printing our books on recycled paper. The paper in every book contains 10% to 30% post-consumer waste (PCW). The cover board on the outside of each book contains 100% PCW. Our goal is to do our part to help young people and the environment too!

Photo Credits: Photo Credits: *Anna* by De Nyselo Turner, oil on canvas, courtesy of The Alan Mason Chesney Medical Archives of The Johns Hopkins Medical Institutions, photo by Aaron Levin, p. 37; Bettmann/Corbis/AP Images, p. 30; Duke University Medical Center Archives, p. 16; Courtesy of The Alan Mason Chesney Medical Archives of The Johns Hopkins Medical Institutions, pp. 3, 21, 24, 28, 32; Courtesy of the Martin Photo Collection at the Iberia Parish Library in New Iberia, image 10,756, p. 8; Courtesy of the Thomas Family and Spark Media, pp. 2, 6, 10; Courtesy of the Vivien Thomas Family, p.17; Life Art image copyright 1998 Lippincott Williams & Wilkins. All rights reserved., pp. 22, 29; Shutterstock.com, pp. 9, 39, 41, 42; *Vivien Thomas* by Bob Gee, oil on canvas, courtesy of The Alan Mason Chesney Medical Archives of The Johns Hopkins Medical Institutions, photo by Aaron Levin, p.34.

Cover Photo: *Vivien Thomas* by Bob Gee, oil on canvas, courtesy of The Alan Mason Chesney Medical Archives of The Johns Hopkins Medical Institutions, photo by Aaron Levin; Shutterstock.com, (Heart).

CONTENTS

1 Where Is Vivien? 7

2 The Dream Becomes a Nightmare 12

3 Partners of the Heart 20

4 To Save a Life 26

5 The Invisible Black Man 33

Timeline 38

You be the Inventor! 39

Words to Know 45

Books and Internet Addresses 46

Index 48

Vivien Thomas

Chapter 1

Where Is Vivien?

The room was dark as night. A door opened. A nurse walked into the darkness. She turned on powerful lights in the operating room. Everything became bright as sunshine. A dozen doctors, nurses, and medical technicians poured into the super-clean room at Johns Hopkins Hospital in Baltimore, Maryland. They checked every medical tool. Nobody talked, because this day was not like any other day. This highly trained team was going to operate on a baby's heart to try to save its life. It was November 29, 1944. The operation had never been done on a person before.

The surgeon, Dr. Alfred Blalock, held out his hand for a very sharp scalpel. He raised it over the baby's chest. Then he stopped and shouted, "Where is Vivien? Go get him."

The man whom Dr. Blalock needed in that operating room was a thirty-four-year-old black researcher named Vivien Theodore Thomas. He was not a medical doctor, and he never would be.

New Iberia, Louisiana, 1910

Carpenter's tools

Vivien was born on August 29, 1910, in New Iberia, Louisiana. His father, William, was a successful carpenter. Before Vivien, the family already had three boys. Mary, his mother, was so sure her next child would be a girl that she named it Vivien before it was born. When boy number four arrived, she kept the name, but changed it to Vivien to make it into a boy's name.

Pearl High School was the only high school for African Americans in North Nashville. Vivien graduated with honors.

In 1912, William and Mary Thomas moved their family to Nashville, a big city in Tennessee. William and his older sons built a comfortable house for the family.

Later on, the teenage Vivien also became a very good carpenter. His father expected Vivien to work with him full-time after finishing high school. Vivien had other ideas. His mind was set on becoming a doctor. That was a very big dream for an African American in those days.

Learning carpentry had taught Vivien how to be careful. He always measured twice so that he would have to cut just once. He never wasted wood, and he never wasted time. Even as a teenager, Vivien began earning good money and started saving for medical school. He graduated with honors from Pearl High School in 1929. He could see his future as a doctor.

Chapter 2

The Dream Becomes a Nightmare

The year 1930 changed Vivien's life. The country was slowing down during the terrible times of the Great Depression. Companies around the country had lost money in the stock market crash. Many people lost their jobs. Banks went out of business. Vivien's bank slammed its doors shut. The bank had lost every dollar Vivien had saved for medical school.

Vivien was out of school and out of work. Then one day a friend took him to meet Dr. Alfred Blalock at Vanderbilt University Medical School in Nashville. The famous and powerful doctor hired him as an assistant in his medical research laboratory.

The 1930s were hard times. Here, people with no jobs wait in line for free food in New York City.

Dr. Alfred Blalock gave Vivien Thomas a job in his research laboratory.

Step by step, the doctor began to trust Vivien with simple research work. Dr. Blalock was impressed with Vivien's skills. The doctor was a great teacher who was always willing to take time to answer questions. But there was another side to Dr. Blalock that Vivien discovered soon enough.

One day, Vivien heard an explosion of words. Dr. Blalock was ranting, raving, and running around knocking down tools. He was screaming out swear words and shouting that nobody ever did anything right. The brilliant doctor thought that Vivien had not kept perfect records of their experiments. He was wild with anger. But he was wrong.

With great sadness, Vivien knocked on Dr. Blalock's office door and asked for his pay. He could not work for a doctor who yelled at him like a crazy man. For Vivien it was a matter of self-respect. He did not complain or explain. He just wanted to leave.

Most of Dr. Blalock's workers suffered through his wild outbursts without saying anything. They would rather risk their pride than risk their job. But Vivien would not stand for it. He walked out.

The brilliant and powerful doctor, who at that time was a "golden boy" of surgery, ran after Vivien and apologized. He promised he would never yell at him again. He kept that promise.

Thomas did many experiments in Dr. Blalock's medical research laboratory.

Clara Beatrice Flanders married Vivien Thomas in December 1933.
The next year, their first daughter was born.

Vivien Thomas and Dr. Blalock were two very different kinds of men, but they shared a love of medical research. Both worked long hours at the hospital without complaining.

Vivien spent nights and weekends building a house in Nashville with his own hands. He met a lovely young woman named Clara Beatrice Flanders and married her on December 22, 1933. Their first girl, Olga Fay, was born the next year. Another girl, Theodosia Patricia, was born four years later.

Thomas with his family, shortly before the move to Baltimore.

Chapter 3

Partners of the Heart

Whenever Vivien asked Dr. Blalock to ask the medical school for a pay raise, the doctor delayed and delayed. Vivien deserved a raise. He was handling difficult experiments. He had learned how to do surgery on laboratory animals. But he faced an endless struggle to support his family on the same low pay a janitor earned. Once more, Vivien told Dr. Blalock that he was being forced to quit. Finally, the doctor got the school to give him a raise. It was not much more money, but it helped.

In 1940, Dr. Blalock took a very important position as head of surgery at the world-famous Johns Hopkins Hospital in Baltimore, Maryland. He asked Vivien to

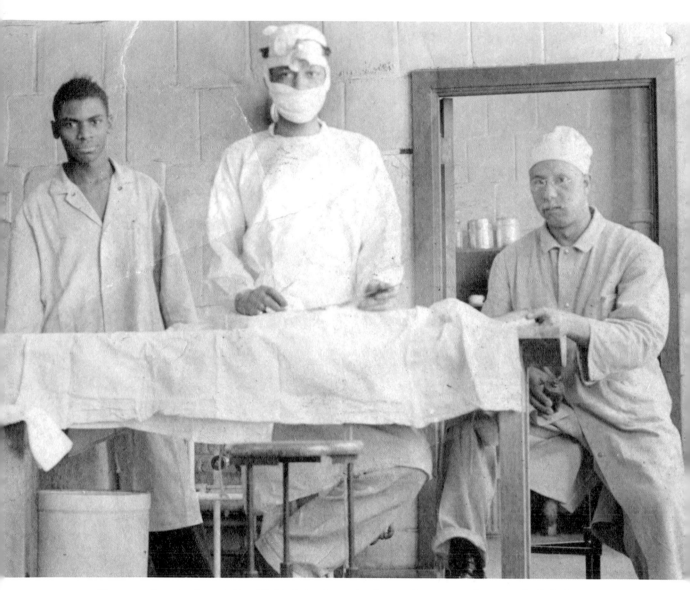

Thomas (center) and Dr. Blalock had worked out the operation on their lab dogs in Tennessee. Although it was for a different problem. "We knew we had the answer," Thomas said.

What Is a Blue Baby?

A blue baby is a child born with a heart that does not pump enough blood to its lungs. The blood of blue babies lacks oxygen, which it should get from the lungs. Blood that lacks oxygen is blue, so their 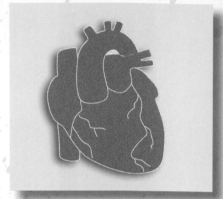 lips, eyelids, fingernails, and toes are blue instead of pink. It hurts them to breathe. When they are old enough to go out and play, even a few slow steps seem to wear them out. Much of the time, these young children sit quietly in bed with their arms folded around their knees. That seems to help them breathe with less pain.

come along as part of his team. Clara and the children moved with him to Baltimore in July of 1941.

The new neighborhood was run down. Vivien's pay was still so low he had to take extra jobs as a bartender to pay his bills. He did not want to leave the hospital, though, because his work there was so interesting. Medical research had become his life.

In 1943, Vivien's world changed again when he and Dr. Blalock met Dr. Helen Taussig, a heart doctor for children. She showed them "blue babies." They were so sick that most did not live very long. Dr. Taussig knew that surgery had never been tried on a human heart. Still, she asked Dr. Blalock and Vivien to find a way to use surgery to keep these children alive.

Other doctors warned Dr. Blalock, Dr. Taussig, and Vivien that nobody should operate on someone's beating heart. This was a basic rule of medicine that those doctors said should not be broken.

Vivien practiced the heart surgery on laboratory dogs. He gave the dogs medicine to prevent pain. Sometimes he had help. Most times, he worked alone. Each operation failed, but each one taught him a new way to operate or the need for a new tool. He created tools that could cut and sew in incredibly tiny spaces. After almost two hundred operations, Vivien, the quiet, careful scientist, operated on a dog named Anna. This little beauty survived. Blood poured through her lungs, giving her life-saving oxygen. Vivien's cutting and stitching were so perfect that Dr. Blalock said they seemed to be "something that the Lord made." The two partners were ready.

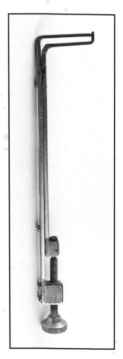

Operating on a heart is very difficult because there is very little room to work. Thomas invented this clamp to help stop bleeding in a very small space.

Dr. Blalock and Vivien studied the problem for months. They decided to close off the heart of a blue baby and cut and move one of the arteries. They would sew the artery to a blood vessel that would send the blood directly to the lungs. Then they would repair the closed-off heart. It would be very dangerous.

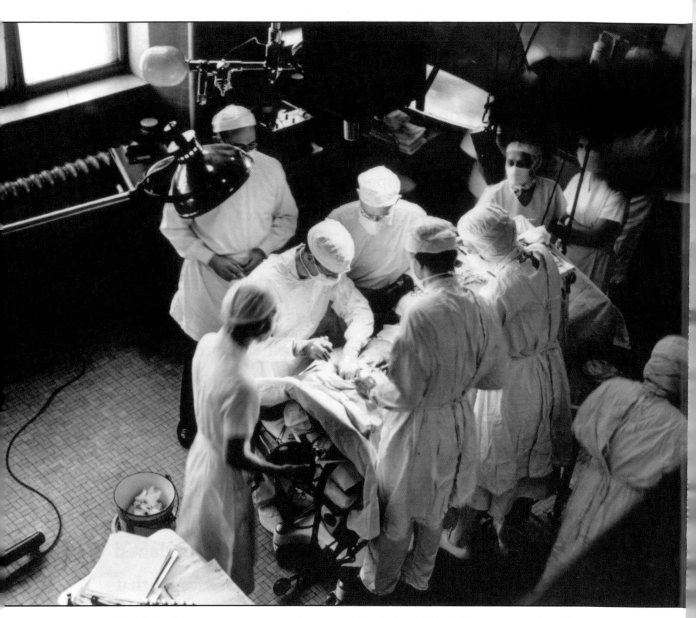

Dr. Blalock is seen here operating on a blue baby. Vivien Thomas stands right behind him.

How Did They Fix a Blue Baby Heart?

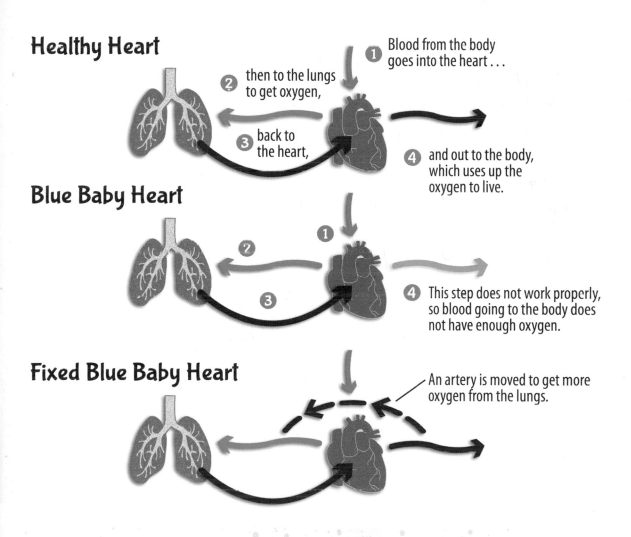

Healthy Heart

① Blood from the body goes into the heart . . .

② then to the lungs to get oxygen,

③ back to the heart,

④ and out to the body, which uses up the oxygen to live.

Blue Baby Heart

④ This step does not work properly, so blood going to the body does not have enough oxygen.

Fixed Blue Baby Heart

An artery is moved to get more oxygen from the lungs.

Diagram of heart surgery

This photo of Dr. Blalock and Dr. Taussig accompanied a newspaper article from the *New York Herald Tribune*. It talked about the two doctors, but left out Thomas.

News of the "blue baby" operations flashed around the world. Parents came cradling blue babies in their arms, begging for help. Vivien assisted Dr. Blalock on the first hundred operations. Magazines and newspapers rushed to Johns Hopkins Hospital to take pictures of everyone on the medical team. But one man's face was always missing from the photos.

Vivien Thomas surprised people when they saw him in a white lab coat. In the 1940s, African Americans were not expected to be doctors.

Chapter 5

The Invisible Black Man

The face of the missing man was black. The laboratory coat he wore was bright white. Vivien Thomas could still remember the first time he walked through the halls of a hospital wearing his white laboratory coat. People had turned to stare. Back then, an African-American man was expected to wear a janitor's uniform, not a white medical coat.

Dr. Blalock had worked one-on-one with Vivien for many years. He depended on Vivien's genius for surgery. But he would not invite him to a celebration party. The doctor could not overcome being raised to believe that one race was better than another. It took a long, long time for

This portrait of Vivien Thomas hangs at Johns Hopkins Hospital today.

many Americans to see the person inside and not the color outside. It is still a problem in the United States today.

Dr. Denton Cooley had been on the team for the first "blue baby" operation. He described Vivien's work by saying, "There wasn't a false move, not a wasted motion when he operated." He remembered, "It was Vivien who had worked it all out in the laboratory, in a dog's heart long before Eileen. . . . There were no heart experts then. That was the beginning." That beginning changed the world of heart surgery. Since then, millions of heart operations have been done, not just on children, but on people of all ages.

Dr. Blalock died in 1964. Vivien Thomas was fifty-four years old then. He would go on running the laboratory for fifteen more years. The man who could not afford medical school later trained hundreds of surgeons.

Johns Hopkins University made Vivien an Honorary Doctor of Laws in 1976. Although he had been teaching medical students for years, he was officially appointed as an instructor of surgery. His portrait was painted and placed in the same hall at Johns Hopkins Hospital as Dr. Blalock's. The two geniuses will be remembered for generations to come.

Also in the halls of Johns Hopkins hangs a portrait of the dog Anna. She was Vivien's first successful patient for the "blue baby" operation. Vivien Thomas, the carpenter who became a scientist, had proved to the world that surgery on a beating heart can be done.

When Anna survived the operation, Thomas knew that his work would be able to help blue babies.

TIMELINE

1910—Vivien Theodore Thomas is born August 29 in New Iberia, Louisiana.

1912— The Thomas family moves to Nashville, Tennessee.

1929—Vivien graduates from Pearl High School, with honors.

1930—Peoples Bank closes its doors. Vivien loses all his savings. He starts work as a laboratory technician for Dr. Alfred Blalock at Vanderbilt University School of Medicine.

1933—Vivien Thomas marries Clara Beatrice Flanders on December 22. They will have two daughters.

1941— Viven Thomas and his family follow Dr. Blalock to Johns Hopkins Hospital in Baltimore, Maryland.

1944—The first blue baby operation, November 29, is successful. Vivien Thomas advises Dr. Blalock step by step through the operation.

1964—Dr. Blalock dies, September 15. Vivien Thomas continues researching and teaching surgery.

1976—Johns Hopkins University awards Vivien Thomas with an honorary degree. He is officially appointed an instructor in surgery, even though he is not a medical doctor.

1979—Vivien Thomas retires from hospital work.

1985—Vivien Thomas dies.

YOU BE THE INVENTOR!

So you want to be an inventor? You can do it! First, you need a terrific idea.

Got a problem? No problem!

Many inventions begin when someone thinks they may have a great solution to a problem. One cold day in 1994, a 10-year-old girl, K.K. Gregory, was building a snow fort. Soon, she had wet, cold snow between her mittens and her coat sleeves. Her wrists became cold and wet from the snow. She found some scraps of fabric around the house, and used them to make a tube that would fit

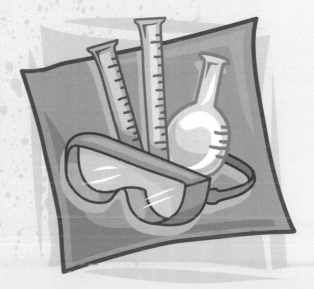

around her wrist. She cut a thumbhole in the tube to make a kind of fingerless glove, and called it a "Wristie." Wearing mittens over her new invention, her wrists stayed nice and warm when she played outside. Today, the Wristie business is booming.

Now it's your turn. Maybe, like K.K. Gregory, you have an idea for something new that would make your life better or easier. Perhaps you can think of a way improve an everyday item. Twelve year-old Becky Schroeder became the youngest female ever to receive a U.S. patent after she invented a glow-in-the-dark clipboard that allowed people to write in the dark. Do you like to play sports or board games? James Naismith, inspired by a game he used to play as a boy, invented a new game he called basketball.

Let your imagination run wild. You never know where it will take you.

Research it!

Okay, you have a terrific idea for an invention. Now what?

First, you'll want to make sure that nobody else has thought of your idea. You wouldn't want to spend hours developing your new invention, only to find that someone else beat you to it. Google Patents can help you find out whether your idea is original.

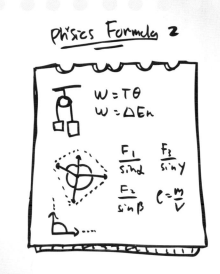

Bring it to life!

If no one else has thought of your idea, congratulations! Write it down in a logbook or journal. Write the date and your initials for every entry you make. If you file a patent for your invention

later, this will help you prove that you were the first person to think of it. The most important thing about this logbook is that pages cannot be added or subtracted. You can buy a bound notebook at any office supply store.

Draw several different pictures of your invention in your logbook. Try sketching views from above, below, and to the side. Show how big each part of your invention should be.

Build a model. Don't be discouraged if it doesn't work at first. You may have to experiment with different designs and materials. That's part of the fun! Take pictures of everything, and tape them into your logbook.

Try your invention out on your friends and family. If they have any suggestions to make it better, build another model. Perfect your invention, and give it a clever name.

Patent it!

Do you want to sell your invention? You'll want to apply for a patent. Holding a patent to your invention means that no one else can make, use, or sell your invention in the U.S. without your permission. It prevents others from making money off of your idea. You will definitely need an adult to help you apply for a patent. It can be a complicated and expensive process. But if you think that people will want to buy your invention, it is well worth it.

GLOSSARY

artery—A large blood vessel that leads into or out of the heart. It carries blood to all the smaller blood vessels.

blood vessel—One of the tubes that carries blood from the heart to the lungs, back to the heart, and then around to all the parts of the body.

carpenter—Someone who works with wood to make things such as chairs, tables, floors, and even whole buildings.

experiment—A very carefully planned test of something that has not been tried before.

medical research—The study of how to help people stay well or get well when they are sick.

medical technician—Someone who is trained to use special tools to help doctors work on patients.

operating room A special spick-and-span room in a hospital with bright lights and all the tools needed for surgery.

oxygen—An part of the air we breathe that is needed to live.

scalpel—A surgeon's knife.

surgeon—A doctor who is specially trained to cut into patients to help cure them.

LEARN MORE

Books

Lester, Julius. *Let's Talk About Race*. New York: HarperCollins Publishers, 2005.

Simon, Seymour. *The Heart: Our Circulatory System*. New York: HarperCollins, 2006.

_____. *Lungs: Your Respiratory System*. New York: HarperCollins, 2007.

To find out more about inventing:

Erlbach, Arlene. *The Kids' Invention Book*. Co., 1997.

St. George, *Judith. So You Want To Be An Inventor?* New York, NY : Philomel Books, 2002.

LEARN MORE

Internet Addresses

To find out more about Vivien Thomas:

In Search of Vivien Thomas
http://www.pubmedcentral.nih.gov

The Network Journal: Vivien Thomas—African American Medical Pioneer's Rise to the Top
http://scripts.tnj.com/lifestyle/black-history/vivien-thomas-honored-johns-hopkins

Footprints Through Time—PBS: Public Broadcasting Service
www.pbs.org/wgbh/amex/partners/legacy/l_colleagues.html

If you want to learn more about becoming an inventor, check out these websites:

Inventnow.org
<http://www.inventnow.org/invent/>

The Inventive Kids Blog
<http://www.inventivekids.com/>

The U.S. Patent and Trademark Office Kid's Pages
<http://www.uspto.gov/web/offices/ac/ahrpa/opa/kids/index.html>

INDEX

A

Anna, the dog, 26, 28

B

Baltimore, Maryland, 5,
15–16
Blalock, Alfred, 5–6, 9–11,
13, 15, 16–17, 19–21, 23,
24, 26, 28
blue baby, 16, 19, 23, 26

C

carpentry, 6, 7–8
clamps, 20
Cooley, Denton, 26

D

Doctor of Laws, 27

F

Flanders, Clara Beatrice
(wife), 13

G

Great Depression, 9

I

instructor of surgery, 27

J

Johns Hopkins Hospital, 5,
15, 23, 27, 28

L

laboratory coat, 25
lungs, 19, 20

M

medical assistant, 9, 19
medical research, 13, 16–17
medical research laboratory,
9, 19, 21, 26

N

Nashville, Tennessee, 7, 9, 13
New Iberia, Louisiana, 6
newspapers, 23

O

operating room, 5–6, 19
operating team, 5, 15, 20, 23,
26
operation, 5, 20, 23, 26, 28

P

pay raise, 15
Pearl High School, 8
portrait
Anna, 28
Blalock, Alfred, 28
Thomas, Vivien, 27

R

racism, 25–26

S

Saxon, Eileen, 19–20
surgery on beating heart, 17,
28
surgical gloves, 19
surgical mask, 29

T

Taussig, Helen, 16–17
Thomas, Mary (mother), 7
Thomas, Olga Fay
(daughter), 13
Thomas, Theodosia
(daughter), 13
Thomas, Vivien
born, 6
died, 28
married, 13
Thomas, William (father),
6–7

V

Vanderbilt University
Medical School, 9